*I just met you Jesus, but I love you.*

Those were my words when Jesus met me at my well. I was *that* woman. A woman of no distinction, of little importance. A woman in my very own town of Sychar; which literally means "drunkenness and falsehood". Although I was never a drunk, I did love marijuana and I definitely lived in my own little world of "me".

And just like that no named woman, who Jesus won over at their encounter at the well…I ran to tell everyone who would listen what had happened! That Jesus loves me for all that I am!

That is how it started for me. I allowed the Lord to use all of my flaws, my experiences, my failures…for His Glory. So He could use my unique story to reach others. That is how one person can and does make a difference.

> Effective evangelism is reaching one person at a time.
> *"Each One, Teach One,"* as I always say.

Matthew 28 speaks, "Jesus, undeterred, went right ahead and gave His charge." I heard that charge. God authorized and commanded me to commission you: *Go out and train everyone you meet, far and near; in this way of life. Mark them by baptism in the threefold name: the Father, the Son and the Holy Spirit. Then instruct them in the practice of all I have commanded you. I'll be with you as you do this, day after day after day…right up to the end of age.*

Notice, it wasn't "suggested" that I to do something. I was commissioned with exact instruction. If you look at the origins of the word commission, it means, "authoritative order, charge, or direction". And believe me, I have been charged!

Women have been targets of the enemy from day one. He knows that we see things that others do not; that women can speak to the heart of issues. The enemy has been tranquilizing women and taking our voices since the beginning, by our own submission or by force from others. There are women, right now that are being mutilated just for being a woman; who are beaten down or don't have a voice of their own. There are cultures that breed woman subjection and these cultures will never change until our voices are returned!

> And this change will take an army…an army of women to rise up and fight alongside men at every battle; to give strength and courage with our solidarity. To win this war!

But first, we as women must be in a place to be able to give. One cannot provide from a place of lack; it must be given from a place of strength and abundance. We all have baggage that we need to unload; baggage of bitterness, un-forgiveness, shame, self-doubt, abuse…fill in the blank. We all have it. But this baggage must be put down…the "place of lack" must be released. After all, as stated in 1 Samuel 1…you will produce what you carry.

Remember, the Lord postponed Hannah's child bearing until she was rid of her bitterness. She could have gone forward with her baggage, but this would have produced a child full of all of the bitterness that filled her. But God loved her too much to leave her the same. So she was changed.

God does His works IN us so that He can do works THROUGH us.

Will you allow God to use you just as you are? Will you put the baggage down, take God's hand and allow Him to supernaturally make something special out of your life?

Picking up this study is a step in that direction. But first a WARNING…You **will** come out a changed woman.

He wants us to be a walking Bible. John 7:38 talks of LIVING WATER. Did you catch that? It said "rivers of LIVING water will flow within them." A living, flowing, walking voice of God.

So, now it's time to get trained women! And remember, we are stronger together. Invite someone to come along on this journey with you. Who will you bring along to share in this journey and be of the living water?

I don't know you, but I love you!

Rachel


*Special Note: Let me say this before we continue: There are NO gender discrepancies in Christ. This is NOT a feminist movement. This is a soul winning movement. Jesus went to the well to win a woman, so she could go evangelize her city to win the men. When the men returned, they brought back lunch. When the woman left the well, she brought back the whole town!*

To my dear friend Robin,
The Lord was showing off when He created you my friend. He blessed my socks off when I prayed for a team to help with this mission when He sent You! I am so excited for this journey, and If I haven't said it before...Thank you for your selflessness, and your big, huge heart! I love you!

To my dear friend Jody,
I love doing life with you! And I am so blessed to have you as a part of this mission! Grab ahold of your socks, because it is going to be an amazing journey! I love you!

# Week 1

# Living into Your Inheritance

## Day 1

**1 John 3:1**

Welcome to the first day of your journey towards freedom and purpose. My goal for you is to really fall in love with the word of God. To find treasures in each scripture and to take the time each day to really meditate on what the Lord may be speaking to you.

What you are going to learn is, HE speaks to us through scripture. And sadly, most people will never hear, because they haven't picked up their Bible to seek the truth.

The journey starts with finding out "who you are" and "whose" you are.

In 1 John 3:1 it states that we are "children of God". The Lord wants you to take this literal. As a matter of fact, we should take all scripture literal, as that was His intention.

Can you wrap your brain around the fact that you are a daughter or a son of a King? Don't worry, it took me years also. But, once you really believe this, the chains that you carry will start to fall off and you will start running, without resistance, towards your dreams and goals.

What are your dreams and goals? Is your journey taking you closer to your fullest potential? Are you realizing all that you are intended to be?

Our identity is not in what we do. If you are a teacher; that is not your identity... that is just what you do. Or, are you a lawyer? Again, not who you are, but what you do.

Let's talk perspective...

As believers, our self-worth is defined in Jesus. The fact is that we are sons and daughters of the King of the most high. We are co-heirs with Jesus Christ. Why are we not living and believing like one?

Paul spoke of this in Romans 8:14-17. Go there now and read those verses. What did Paul say about the Holy Spirit and its role in our lives in these verses?

In Galatian's 3:26-27, read these verses then re-write this verse below.

✧ **What action makes us "son's and daughter's" of Christ?**

Now let's take a look at Galatians 4:6-7

> **What do you think was meant by "no longer a slave, but a son, since you are a son, God has made you also an heir"?**

In those times, in Rome, an adopted child was guaranteed all legal rights to his father's property, even if he was formerly a slave. He was equal to all sons, even the biological, blood heirs.

As adopted sons and daughters of God, we are co-heir's with Christ. We claim all the freedom He has provided to and for us.

> So, if we believe we are co-heirs of Christ, and abundant living is our inheritance...why do some of us not live into that life?

I read a story about a boy who was born without arms...who also happens to be the 10th best archer in the world. Yes, you saw that correct; world ranked archer, with no arms. When asked how he had accomplished such an astounding feat, he stated that "it's all about belief".

I would bet a million bucks that his parent's never told him that he was handicapped, or that he would not be able to do certain things because of his lack of arms. I would suspect that they never spoke death over his future, but rather spoke love and encouragement. In truth, he probably didn't know that he shouldn't be able to do the things that he accomplished.

To the critical eye, there is no way someone without any arms could even hold a bow, let alone be one of the best in the world. Isn't belief an amazing gift!

Another example of exceling on pure belief is the lovely bumble bee. Did you know, anatomically speaking, the bumble bee should not be able to support its own weight and be able to fly. But don't you know…that bubble bee doesn't know that it isn't supposed to be able to fly! He just believes and takes off!

On my journey, I decided to break the yoke of speaking death over my family. I am a work in progress, as we all are. But I knew that I had to address this in myself as a priority. I know and believe that we become who the most important person in our life thinks that we are. This is called the glass theory and I have seen if fulfilled over and over again. So, I vowed to take control, to become the CEO of my home and speak life and encouragement over my entire family. I chose to provide an environment for my kids to keep their "child- like faith" and enable them to believe in themselves. My family is the most important people in my life and I would BE the person that I wanted them to see in me. Belief leads to action which brings about reality.

If you change the way you see yourself, you can change your world.

Describe the person that you want others to see in you:

God's dream for you is the enemy's nightmare. The enemy does not want you to know who you are! Often times the enemy knows who we are before we do. The enemy does not want to see us become what God has intended...that is the enemy's worst nightmare. One of our prime battles is to recognize the enemy and be prepared!

Take it from me and my personal experiences in fighting the enemy...he is relentless...especially when we are on the right path. Know that when you start this journey, the attacks are going to come. But, the enemy doesn't attack you for who you are now, or who you used to be; but rather, who you might become in the future.

So keep in mind:

1. If you are a Christian, you are a target. Satan has your name... and he's watching you. It's his job to derail your journey. Just remember that it's not personal, it's just good business for him to attack those on the right path
2. You have not fulfilled your full destiny. God has given you an inheritance that entitles you to be more. But it requires action. You can either BE the hero or NOT be the hero. The choice is yours. But I know this...God has filled you with potential. It is your job to choose to become who God has intended. Become the person you want others to see in you! You are a hero. It's time to rise up with the attitude that you are a hero waiting to happen...and you are READY!

## Day 2

**Jeremiah 17:14**

Can you recall the first time you had your heart broken? Many of our broken hearts occurred early in life, at least that is when I experienced my first. There are so many scriptures that address this very thing. And for good reason! Heart break is a burden carried by us all at many points in our life. Of course, God knew this and that is why he provided so many answers on how to heal in the best self-help book ever created: the BIBLE (Basic Instructions Before Leaving Earth).

Read Isaiah 61:1.

We must remember that this prophecy was written about 700 years before the birth of Christ our Lord.

Who do you think Isaiah was referring to when he said, "He sent me to bind up the broken hearted?"

Now let's go to Luke 4:16-27   Read this out loud.

Refer back to Isaiah to get some clarity. During the time of Isaiah, what Isaiah had prayed for, did not get delivered, or at least to the expectation that he had. After the release of the Babylonian exile, the people remained conquered and oppressed and not free at all.

Isaiah was more than likely speaking of the Messianic age. As Jesus stated, "Today this scripture is fulfilled in your hearing."

Now let's talk about the WHY He does not meet our every expectation and He allows us to have heartbreak. In Isaiah 66:9, New Century version, it says this, "I will not cause pain without allowing something new to be born," says the Lord. 'If I cause you the pain, I will not stop you from giving birth to your new nation,' says your God."

- **What does this verse mean to you? Write down your thoughts or new insights to this?**

Can you remember a time when you lost a loved one, or maybe that loved one died in a horrible way, maybe even lost someone to suicide? And you were left almost mad at God?

- **Think about that for a minute then I want you to now look at your life now, and reflect on the new things that were birthed from that tragedy.**

The enemy will use tragedy as an opportunity to distract you from God's path. He wants you to become upset, to make you weaker... and to even get you to blame God for your pain.

But let's look at what the truth says, "The thief comes only to steal and kill and destroy; I have come that they may have life and have it more abundantly!" John 10:10

The enemy is an embezzler of our faith...of our goodness. What does an embezzler do? They steal slowly over time, taking this piece now...taking that piece later...until eventually everything that is good will all be gone.

But we will be armed with God's guidance and shut down the embezzler!

Are you starting to see why it is so important to know what the word of God says? His word is our weapon to fight the enemy. Each time the enemy spouts out the lies, we have been armed and can come back with His truth to put the enemy in his place!

The enemy seeks out all of our weakness to use against us. One of our greatest weaknesses are our wounds. We must do all that we can to heal these wounds and close these opportunities to the enemy.

Take a moment and identify your greatest wound.

What is it that costs you the most pain? This wound will be your new calling. The Lord will use it to connect with others...to "bind up the brokenhearted" in a BIG WAY.

But, will you answer the call?

The first step is healing the wound. This starts by identifying the source of the pain, remembering that you are co-heirs with Christ, and then start the process of pruning the wound. Face it head on and take away its power over you.

Rid yourself of all of the un-forgiveness, bitterness, shame and any other stronghold that this wound holds over you. Look to God, release the pain and BE FREE!

# Day 3

**2 Corinthians 5:17**

I want to start day 3 with a story. Well, not really a story, but a metaphor that will help you see that when you say YES to Jesus, that you truly are made a new.

Picture a large farm on a warm, late summer afternoon. You can hear the chickens clucking, the sheep talking to each other...you can feel the warm sun on your cheeks.

You look to your right and see a pumpkin patch. Got the image in your head? Good! Now picture God sees the same thing, only as He looks down...those pumpkins are us!

First, God scans the pumpkin patch, reaches down...picks you and brings you in from the field. The Bible says He selects us out of the world. Just like we pick a pumpkin out of its patch.

> Once picked, we are in the world, but no longer of the world.

He then washes all of the "dirt" off of our outside. The dirt that we picked up being around all of the other pumpkins...all of the outside influences from our former lives that must be cleaned up. The old is cleaned away, allowing all things to become new.

Then, ever so carefully, He removes all of the "yucky stuff" we call "sin" out from our inside. With a single gesture, the sin is gone!

He carefully removes all those seeds of doubt, hate, greed, and fear. He replaces them with the seeds of Faith, Hope and Love. After you invite Jesus inside, you begin to experience the changing power of God's love in your life. Sin will no longer hold such power over us!

God then looks at His clean pumpkin...holding it gently in his hands. Smiling down on each of us. In that very instance, simply by His presence in our lives...our faces are carved a new! Our gratitude becomes so great, it will literally show on our face!

Our love for Him becomes so great, it is as if a candle has been lit on our inside. Look! We radiate just like a jack o' lantern with the light of God!

So too, when Jesus (who is called the Son of Light) lives inside of us; He shines through our life for all to see. His light reflects through us to reveal His presence.

"Let your light so shine before men that they may be able to see your good works and glorify your Father, who is in heaven."


So you see, we Christians are really just like the pumpkin! Once we are picked, cleaned and loved...we will never be the same with Jesus inside of us. As the candle is to the jack o' lantern, "Thy presence, my light!"


If you have not accepted Jesus into your heart, stop what you are doing, and do it NOW. It doesn't have to be fancy, just a simple, "Lord, I need you, please forgive my sins, come into my heart, I'll make you my Lord and savior."

That just secured your entrance into heaven.

You're welcome!

(notes)

Read today's scripture (2 Corinthians 5:17).

> **If you have been saved, write down things about your old self that are no longer present.**

For me, I was a complete 180! Just like the un-named woman at the well... I went from habitual liar, to always telling the truth. I was a complete procrastinator, and now I go get it! I don't sit on the fence, I just go! I have gained so much more ground in these last 10 years then I did in my first 35 years.

And let me tell you...when I was born again, people noticed. I mean, I had the same clothes on, but I looked different. It was really almost an unbelievable transformation. People would say about me, or would constantly remind me of the past with things like: "Rachel? A Christian? She was the wildest girl of them all? Rachel a Christian? She was a ho!"

BUT, no one could deny the light shining out of me.

I got caught in that trap in the beginning. You know, when the one's closest to you want to point out how you used to be, or maybe just can't wrap their brain around it, so they still treat you the same? That is the enemy! He is the one who yells all of our sins to us and will use those closest to you to do it. This is going to happen. Just be ready for it. But with time, you will really embrace WHO YOU ARE, and WHOSE YOU ARE. You'll know the truth, and the truth will really set you FREE.

But the enemy will accuse...

And when the accuser tries to pull me back down, I will say, "Well, that's a lie!" I respond with the word of God, and I will likely quote 2 Corinthians 5:17: "Therefore, if anyone is in Christ, the new creation has come: The old has gone, the new is here!"

Oh and then I will tell him where to go!

- **How did you feel after reflecting on your old self? Did you feel sad, or anxious, or did you feel grateful that you are new? Be honest.**

God will use you right where you are, your flaws, your experiences, your failures, ALL OF IT! We are not re-formed or re-educated, or rehabilitated. We are actually recreated.

We are not just turning over a new leaf, but a new life with a new Father!

So, you have a choice. Will you allow the Lord to supernaturally make something special out of your life?

# Day 4

**Matthew 6:25-27**

In Philippians chapter 4, Paul wrote about not being anxious or worrying about anything. I looked the word "anything" up in Greek and it literally means ANYTHING. I like to paraphrase the verse like this: "If you are going to pray, don't worry, but if you are going to worry, don't pray". We all struggle at some point with letting go and letting God take our burdens. I think this has much to do with the control that we as humans think we have. We carry around all of this junk. It weighs us down. It makes us bitter. It makes us unbearable to be around. It sucks the life out of our lives! But yet we still hang on to it, pretending that we are in control.

Read Luke 12:11.

⋄ **Put yourself in the disciple's shoes for a minute. What would your response be if you were faced with this leap of faith?**




Early in "my walk" with God, I really didn't grasp all that came with being a believer. I was a believer, but I wasn't receiving. I knew about the Holy Spirit, but I really didn't know about all of the power that comes with that Holy Spirit. There is power in releasing your worries to God. It all goes back to the praying and then not worrying, right?

Now look at Matthew 10:17.

This time there was more at stake and very heavy circumstances. Flogging? I don't know about you, but flogging sounds really painful.

But read on through Matthew 10:19. "...do not worry about what to say or how to say it. At that time you will be given what to say." Again, Jesus was affirming that the Holy Spirit would intercede for them. Jesus has our backs!

I feel like the Lord wants me to help you hear from the Holy Spirit. I believe that is why I am on the Earth...and why you picked up this study.

God brings us what we need when we need it, if we would only see.

But Faith can be a scary thing sometimes; especially when it's a life or death or a painful situation. Faith explores what revelation reveals.

➤ **Think about a time when you had to make a very important decision in your life. What were the circumstances, and what was your path in making that decision? Write down all things including people you may have reached out to for guidance.**

1 Peter 5:7 says "cast ALL your _____ on Him because \_\_\_\_ _____ _____ _____."

I looked up the word ALL in Greek also, and guess what it means? Yep! It means ALL!!!

James 1 says that when you persevere you build Faith. Often times, God will not meet you at that moment of perseverance. God does not want to meet you at the moment of crisis or at church when they do an altar call. He doesn't want to build a moment of connection only where you have to get to the same place to connect again.

What He does want is to connect with you in those moments of perseverance…at 1 AM, when you get down on your knees in your bedroom to speak to Him; or He will meet you on your drive to the church for that altar call.

Our Lord is a leader. He wants to make us leaders, to enable us. He wants to give us the tools that will enable us to grow up in HIM and not dependent upon a very specific environment for those connections.

History tells us that we will get through our trials. This is the promise of James 1.

"Let _____ finish its work so that you may be mature and complete, not lacking anything."


This is the glory of building a history in God. This is why every time you get mad, or go through trials, you must stick it out and say, "I'm not leaving this place. I'm going to build a history with you! Tell me your truth, and tell me your promises."

This is how you go from believing to knowing. This is how you build character, marriages, businesses. This is how you deal with pain, you don't run. This is how you grow in God!

# Day 5

**Mark 12: 41-44**

As I am writing this, I am sitting outside on my back deck that has been beautifully decorated because of a vision I had that has been realized. My view is of abundant, green trees and a beautiful lake. I am blessed to be able to sit on this deck, with this view and watch the sun rise every morning and set every evening.

I know in my heart that I would not be this blessed if I had not followed the guidance found in the Bible about money and giving.

In Proverbs 11:24-25 : "There is one who scatters, and yet increases all the more, and there is one who withholds what is justly due, and yet it results only in want. The generous man will be prosperous, and he who waters will himself be watered."

My journey may have started out a little different than some of yours, but some can relate directly. I am sure I am not the only person out there who was SO broken that I ran straight into Jesus' arms and gave it ALL up to Him. I was broken, busted and disgusted. And I got that way, because of my selfish, "what's in it for me", worldly ways.

Read 2 Kings 12:9-12

> **What thought comes to your mind when reading this?**

Here are my thoughts: We are the hands and feet of Jesus. We are his only bank account. There is no denying that in our society, we require cash to ensure certain needs are met. Without meeting these needs, our ability to reach the masses and spread the word of Jesus is very limited.

So think about your church. How do you think the light bill is paid? How are the people who run the church paid?

Our tithes and offerings directly support the infrastructure needed to build the Kingdom. It isn't about building more brick, or buying more chairs, necessarily. These things are necessary to support the congregation. But it is all about supporting the mission.

But what is tithing exactly?

Well, "tithe literally" means a tenth or 10%. This is commonly accepted as the percentage of your household intake that should be given, either in tithes or offerings.

So why do you think we are expected to tithe?

I believe that tithing was ultimately a tool used to teach us to be better people. Think about it...freely giving teaches us how to be unselfish by putting other's needs before our own. Unselfish people make better friends, workers, spouses, moms, dads, children and on and on. And in this we learn one of God's lessons...to be patient, give and reward will be provided in time.

Read Luke 21:1-2.

In contrast to the wealthy giving tokens of their wealth, the poor widow gave all she had to live on...two coins. She gave all that she had because she believed.

Some people will put a $20 in the offering plate and think that is good. Sure, that is good if all that came into your house that week was $200. But it falls a little short if your house brought in $2000. As the Bible guides us, you will receive back what you offer freely. Don't limit your blessings by holding back what you are capable of providing.

You need proof? That's easy enough...just do it. Tithe freely, give freely without expectation. Then keep your eyes open to witness!

Malachi 3:10: "Test me in this," says the Lord Almighty, "and see if I will not throw open the floodgates of heaven and pour out so much blessing that there will not be room enough to store it."

> As you sow, so shall you reap.

- **I want you to be honest right now with yourself and take some moral inventory. Write down your feelings on giving and tithing.**

Has this changed after reading this day's discussion?

Keep an open heart, don't disregard the guidance provided to us by His word and be open to all the blessings intended for you.

Your challenge this week:

Tithe the income that comes into your hands / household.

And tithe from the gross, not the net. Think about it, do you want a gross blessing or a net blessing?

I can guarantee this…

God will NOT bless you with more if He can't trust you with a little.

(notes)

# Week 2

# Since I Got the Call, No More Saul...Now I'm Paul!

## Day 1

**Act 2:14-20**

In this verse, Peter was talking about the Holy Spirit. He was referring to the Power that we receive as followers of Jesus Christ. Christ is the cornerstone of our salvation, but the Holy Spirit is the agent of transformation. Peter, before and without Jesus, was unstable and he often let his bravado be his downfall. The NEW, transformed Peter was humble, yet BOLD, but this new confidence came from the Holy Spirit. When he spoke, it was the Holy Spirit that made him a powerful and dynamic speaker.

In verses 17-21, Peter was testifying to the fact that when we take on the Holy Spirit, which means accepting Jesus as our Lord and savior, we take on a power! WE will start to dream and have visions, which will all come from the Holy Spirit.

Vision is what we see, but it is also the WAY in which we see. Vision is the lens that interprets the events of our life, the way we view people and our concept of God. If we have a scratch on our glasses, it may seem like everybody around us has scratches too. But the problem actually lies with us, because our vision is impaired.

Jesus said that our eyes are the windows of our heart. Paul prayed that the eyes of our heart would be enlightened.

In other words, Paul prayed that we would *perceive* with our eyes

but we *see* with our hearts.

Our minds receive images from our eyes, but our heart is our interpreter. If our heart becomes bitter, jealous, hurt or in some way infected; the lens of our heart is distorted….just like the scratched lens on your glasses. What we perceive is happening and what is really going on could be two completely different things.

Jesus said, "You will know the truth and the truth will make you free" (John 8:32).

The word truth used here is not referring to the Bible itself, (although all truth is rooted in the Bible). In this quote, the word truth means reality. Jesus is saying, you will understand what is real and that will free you.


So many of us live in a kind of virtual reality. The way we view life can feel and look real, or make perfect sense, but still not be real at all. Have you ever watched a good movie and gotten totally into it? I do this all of the time. I fall into the characters and can literally feel what they are feeling. You can experience all of the emotions of real life. You may even leave the theater still "feeling" the movie, but it was just a movie, right? It was never real.

The truth is: we see what we believe to be true in the framing or setting in which we saw it. A different framing or setting changes what it is we see. Another way to put it is; if you have the wrong pretext, you will misunderstand the context.

Having a revelation of what is really real, will deliver us from a life of torment that this misperceived virtual reality often causes.

Read John 8:27-32

- **Write down some examples of cliché's or out of context ways that you have heard people have used this verse:**

John 8:32, "Then you will know the truth, and the truth will set you free."

Let me just preface this by saying, to tell a lie is wrong. There is no way for a lie to be the right answer. Plus, my Momma always told me that you should always tell the truth; because when you tell you truth, you never have to remember what you said.

This is so true. But I also think that Jesus was not saying, "Just tell the truth, and you will be free". Yes, that is true: telling the truth will free you. After all, lies are just a form of bondage. But, what Jesus meant is that HE, is the only way to heaven. He was speaking to his disciples and wanted to make sure that they knew that He was the only way to freedom and to an abundant life.

> The Holy Spirit IN us is always working.
> Always trying to communicate with us. He is always trying to affirm us.

Our freedom is a life of abundance, peace and love found through Him. If you don't have a vision for your life, then just ask the Father for a vision. Ask Him questions. If you don't get your answer, then ask a new question. You will know when you are on the right path...for He will affirm you!

Another tool for your toolbox: Fasting

According to Wikipedia, fasting is a willing abstinence or reduction from some or all food, drink, or both, for a period of time.

Fasting has been a powerful tool used in Christian disciplines to bring you closer to God, to unclutter your mind to hear His words and allow the Holy Spirit to transform your life.

Fasting can bring about an untapped clarity to your vision, your path, your journey.

I use this tool daily, as part of my spiritual journey. Along with yoga, fasting has quieted my voice so I can hear His and receive a clearer vision. I will continue to include fasting as part of my walk. It has changed everything.

Your action steps:

- **I want you to fast tomorrow morning! Don't eat your first meal until 1 or 2 pm. In this time, every time you feel any sense of hunger, I want you to pray and meditate. Begin to ask your questions to your loving Father in Heaven.**

Be patient…listen…and He will affirm you!

# Day 2

**Matthew 21:18-22**

Think about when you were a kid. Do you remember how confident and sure you were about your answer when you were asked, "What do you want to be when you grow up?"

I have had the opportunity to chaperone several field trips with 3rd and 4th graders, while serving at my two youngest children's school. And I love to ask this question!

I am always tickled with their responses. They will shout with confidence, "I want to be a professional baseball player!" or, "I don't know, but I want to make a lot of money!"

I have also come across the 10-year-old who has already experienced a dark, skeptical world and no longer has any belief. Someone in their life has stolen their ability to dream. Adults do this without really knowing the consequences of their actions. "You can't be an engineer, you're not good enough in math." "A star on Broadway? Come back to Earth!" I've even heard teachers yell at a kid staring out of the window and telling them to "stop daydreaming".

Jesus tells us that we have the authority to write or own stories.

I take this literally. I will write my story...He will guide me, inspire me, bring me the resources that I need. But I will dream and it will be so.

Look back at Matthew 17:20

Jesus speaks to his disciples in regard to why they couldn't cast the demon out of the boy, "Because you have so little faith. Truly I tell you, if you have faith as small as a mustard seed, you can say to this mountain, 'Move from here to there,' and it will move. Nothing will be impossible for you.

Jesus is our inherited power. With Him we can do…well, we can do anything!

> But we must LISTEN to His words and have Faith.

Think about how Jesus must have felt at times…providing answers, but His words falling on deaf ears.

- **Write down what you would feel like if someone was always asking for your guidance, but never took action?**

Thank the Heaven's that God's patience is eternal! And he will not give up on us, even if he has to show us over and over before we listen!

Let's look at Mark 11:22-25

Mark 11: 24 "Therefore I tell you, whatever you _____ _____ _____ _____, believe that you have _____ it, and it will be yours."

In order to pray effectively and see your prayer's manifest, you must first ask and then have faith in the Lord!

The Lord will only say NO if a "yes" violates your purpose. But be assured...He is truly looking out for you. Like any good Father, He is protecting you... and He has something bigger and better in mind.

Read Matthew 7:7

> **What do you think this verse is referring to? Write down your answers:**

One of my favorite Bible verses of all times is Matthew 6:33, "seek ye first the Kingdom and all these things will be added unto you".

Remember, this is our instruction manual. You must first seek the Kingdom. Listen and follow the guidance provided.

In Matthew 7:7, Jesus is telling us to next pursue the Father. But, oh my...this will take persistence!

"Ask and it will be given to you; seek and you will find; knock and the door will be opened to you."

Think about when you first starting dating your spouse. Did you fall in love on the first date? Of course not! It took some time and many dates before you really knew who your spouse was as a person and who you were with them. This didn't happen over night...in many cases it could have taken years; or is still happening. After all a good marriage is a journey traveled together.

The journey to know the Father is the same. Even more than you want a relationship with Him; He desires to be in relationship with you as well!

Our Father wants to give us the desires of our hearts. He wants us to be happy, to be fulfilled, to be at peace. It says in scripture that "he will supply all our needs according to His glorious riches". So, see...you need not worry about how you are going to buy clothes, pay your mortgage, or feed your family. The verse states clearly that those things will be provided abundantly! But you have to kick things off...just start telling the Father what you want and He will provide!

# Day 3

**Matthew 4:18-20**

I have a confession. The story in my book "How Jesus and Yoga changed my life" about my encounter at the Mickey Mouse headstone was about 2 years ago from the time of this writing. He told me plain and clear, "I want you to do what I told the disciples to do in the great commission".

Since that day, I have been striving to bring this command to realization. I have had success in applying this charge to our businesses. But I know in my heart that bringing this message to our businesses is not all that I was put me on this earth to do.

I have been fasting and praying a lot lately about The Mission. You know, my purpose...what God wants me to accomplish in His name.

When I am provided tools to add to my "walk", I use them. I have learned to listen and follow the guidance as it is provided. This includes my recent addition of fasting as part of my journey.

> Dieting changes the way you look, but fasting changes the way you see.

Lately, I have been asking lots of questions. And just as I have guided you to do... if I don't hear from the Father, I simply ask another question.

Yesterday morning I was having a conversation with my husband, Curt. He reminded me of something that I often talk about and actually shared in my writing as well....

My ministry will come from my greatest wound.

My greatest wound has been not having my Earthly dad present in my life. Due to this lack of presence, I was one very lost soul! The very epitome of The Woman at the Well.

During this conversation, Curt followed by asking, "but where's your heart?" Wow...what a great question! But I knew the answer...my passion is to stop the demoralization of women in this world. I know for a fact that many of the women who are struggling in their lives or are on paths they wouldn't have otherwise chosen...such as stripper's, porn stars, drug addicts or engage in derogatory acts for one reason or another; sometimes to even get the drugs that control them. Many of these women found these paths because they also did not have a father figure in their life. Or, they were violated or betrayed by a man or woman as a child. Some of these damaged women have even been in and out of jail over the course of their lives.

These women have absolutely NO idea that they are actually royalty!

They are daughters of the one true King. They don't understand that the junk they carry with them make them a slave to their current lifestyle. They have no idea that they have been bestowed with the power and authority to be truly FREE!

Let's go to Roman's 8:17

"Now if we are children, then we are heirs—heirs of God and co-heirs with Christ, if indeed we share in his sufferings in order that we may also share in his glory."

Read that again…"if indeed we share in his sufferings in order that we may also share in His glory."

Along with being Heir's with Jesus, comes power…supernatural power. When we allow our spirit to guide us; when we fast and pray, we *will* see the supernatural!

But with great rewards comes great responsibility. All things will be in balance…along with the power and the blessings, will come suffering.

I told a story in my book, early in my walk where I was just sick and tired, of being sick and tired. I am sure some of you can relate! I had taken all that I could when It came to dealing with the person my husband was at the time. There were too many struggles to share here. Just trust me, we were in a dark place.

But, I was ALL IN Jesus by this time. And I was willing to be obedient, even if that meant staying in that particular suffering if it was for His glory. Can I be honest? Man, that really sucked! But I knew what I had to do…After all, Jesus suffered beyond understanding.

He reminded me of His suffering and asked me to compare mine to His. Then He reminded me that His suffering was the price he paid for me to be FREE indeed!

So, I stuck it out. I prayed a lot. I listened when God provided guidance and now, I have the marriage that I always desired!

Go now to Romans 8:18

Jesus actually led me to this verse in during these moments. This verse was a huge shift for me...

It gave me perspective that allowed me to pick myself up and keep on going. And it only made me dig deep and reveal how strong I really am. After all, the toughest people are those who have endured the most pain, but are still smiling.

Let's get more confirmation, look at 2 Corinthians 4:17

One of the the tactics that Satan uses is that he will start telling you lies. He will bombard you with so many awful things that they will manifest in offense and complaints. He will get us to focus on everyone and everything else, versus the truth. Remember the voice of the Lord is a singular, small whisper. The enemy will try to get you to lose your faith. But we have tools to combat this battle strategy.

We must realize that with every pain, there is a new birth waiting to happen. It's is all about perspective. Remember, our perception shapes our reality.

- **Can you recall a situation where you were experiencing some Spiritual warfare, but you felt the presence of the Lord?**

# Day 4

**Luke 8:26-39**

An area of bondage that I carried throughout most of my life, well up until my conversion with Jesus at the well, was trying to be something I was not. I had NO idea who I was or *whose* I was. Looking back now, even I can't believe some of the things that I did! I was the Wild Child...lost...searching...trying to be something that I wasn't. But even so, I know without a doubt, that now I am so much better than everyone or everything I was trying to be back then.

I know that I am even changed from who I was 3 years ago, 2 years ago or even last year. With every step on my walk, I am again a new person.

I have been on this journey ever since I said YES to Jesus. And a journey is exactly the point...this is an every growing, rediscover yourself at every turn kind of thing.

My transformation was not exactly like the demon possessed man being freed of his captor, but I believe that I did have some evil spirits in me that were keeping me from Jesus. The enemy knew me all too well. And he knew that I had the potential destiny to be a world changer...and once I was in, I would be ALL IN with Jesus.

Read and compare Matthew 8:29 and Mark 5:7-20

- **What are the similarities' and what are the differences?**

What I love most about the Bible is that many of the disciples had similar experiences with Jesus, but all shared different versions of the experience. But the experience and outcome remained the same. Some disciples just elaborated a little more than others or provided their perspective or view of the events.

For example: in Matthew 8:28 - 32, Matthew conveys simply of a man possessed by an evil spirit. But in Mark 5:7-20, Mark depicts the details of the occurrence and he has same account as Matthew; but he goes on to document what happened "after" the demon is cast out. One occurrence, two slightly different focuses on the events. This allows us to compare the event from multiple perspectives to gain the most from the experience.

2 Corinthians 5:17, "Therefore, if anyone is in Christ, the new creation has come: The old has gone, the new is here!"

Sometimes I think that the Lord chooses some the most messed up people to champion His word! But honestly, think about that...what better way for us to connect with others so that they will really hear His messages.

He has a plan and purpose for all of our struggles and will use all of them so that we can continue in His mission. Besides, if we were all perfect, then what would the glory be in that?

Take a second look at 2 Corinthians 5:17

Write down all the things that are no longer "in you" because you became NEW in Christ.

I needed 2 pages to fill mine out, but that is greater GLORY to Him! Being new in Christ means you are re-created, not just rehabilitated.

Read Revelation 21:4-5

Some may think it is morbid to I think about death. But, I don't really think about death any more than I think about eternity.

What are your thoughts and feelings are as you read this passage?

Furthermore, I want you to really meditate on it. Think about what a "new Jerusalem" would be like. I am asking you to daydream about what NEW would look like for you.

Are there still some things in your past you haven't shared with anyone? Something that may be causing you to feel shame? If there are, you gotta let them out!
If you don't' have a trusted person, go see a Christian counselor and get it out. The enemy loses all control and power when we face our shortcomings and confess.

# Day 5

**Colossians 3:15-17**

Every morning, soon after I wake up for the day, I try to get myself into a grateful state. It isn't hard for me, because the Lord has blessed me so much. It is easier for me in this stage of my life to identify my blessings and get my head in the right place to be grateful for them all. But this wasn't always the case. It took lots of effort to get here and it takes effort to keep myself here.

But I do this to get me going on a positive note as soon as I can in the morning, so the rest of my day flows on positivity. I believe thankful people have the right perspective to worship wholeheartedly. Being grateful will open our hearts to the Lord's peace and enables us to move forward with LOVE.

- **So here is an interesting question: What do you see when you see a donut?**

Did you answer "a hole"? Yep, me too! I had a 9-year-old school me on my error in perception and pointed out that I was seeing things all wrong. Her wise 9 years corrected me and said, "You focused on what wasn't there, instead of what was there!" What a great "in your face and calling you out" moment. God speaks through us all to teach His word...even sweet little girls!

Read Ephesians 5:19-20 and list the things we are to do as followers of Jesus.

2 years ago my husband, Curt, and I took all 4 of our children on a 7-day cruise. I had dreaded the thought of taking my kids on a cruise for year's! All over stupid fears! Like, one of these crazy fears was that someone would fall off of the boat. Now, is that of the enemy or what? Lies, doubt and fear...he was using them all to keep me from having a life experience with my family.

I know now that it was all the enemy and his voice in my ear that kept me from wanting to take our children with us.

Over the years, my husband and I have taken many cruises. But I gotta tell you...the cruise that we took as a family was the best one yet.

On this family cruise, we met a wonderful woman, Sunita. She took care of us every night at dinner, so we got to know her more each day. We found out that most of the people who worked on the boat were from other countries. Many sacrificed months away from family to do what had to do to get a step ahead and provide for their loved ones. Sunita worked 7 months a year on the boats...she was missing time with her child to invest in their future. Her goal was to work hard now and then go back home and buy a house for her and her family. A real home instead of the grass hut they lived in now. We learned so much from Sunita, especially when it came to gratitude. Even in her time of sacrifice, she was appreciative of every opportunity that came her way.

We learned so much from Sunita…what true gratitude really was. And I got to teach her a little something too! I shared Jesus with her! I also shared a scripture that has been the truth in my own life.

Go to Joel 2:25

> **What things in your life has the enemy temporarily stolen from you?**

Now, write down the things that have been restored

God's word promises our restoration. In Isaiah 25:1, Isaiah honored and praised God because he realized that God always completes his plans as promised.

And as in Luke 1:45, "He will always fulfill His promises to you."

Think about all the prayer's He has answered, and praise Him for His faithfulness!

# On Earth, as it is in Heaven

(notes)

# Week 3

# On Earth As It Is In Heaven

## Day 1

**1 Corinthians 12:4-11**

I recently sent out a survey to my mailing list and asked some very hard questions. One of the questions I posed: "Do you wake up every morning juiced about life everyday".

95% of the responses were "NO".

Another question I asked was: "Do you know why you are here on earth". And the same 95% responded with a "NO".

We humans have a tendency to overcomplicate things. Believe me, I am one of them! I used to make everything harder than it had to be. We have to remind ourselves NOT to overcomplicate what is intended to be so simple.

Do we really think the Lord wants us wondering around in a never-ending maze trying to figure all of this out?

I know that sometimes I feel that way. When this happens, I take a moment to reflect on the struggle. Then I realized I just wasn't asking the right questions to the Lord!

He makes it pretty simple, but it is our flesh (and our overthinking minds) that gets in our way.

(notes)

Let's take a look at our scripture for today: **1 Corinthians 12:4-11**

Now, write below the things that you are really good at and very passionate about when you are doing them.


Now, it's time for a quick, fun test. Go to <u>www.spiritualgiftstest.com.</u> Don't worry, it's easy and you can't answer anything incorrectly.

> **What were your top 3 gifts? How do they compare to what you listed above? Are you surprised?**


Remember, all who are in Christ have the Holy Spirit, but the Holy Spirit decides which gifts each believer should have.

My top 3 gifts have changed over the years, and that is expected as our experiences change us. But the ones that have been in the top have been pretty consistent. Teaching, Leading and exhortation have always shown up as my gifts. This just shows that I am still on the path God has intended. I am so blessed!

So now, we have identified what "gets us juiced" and what we are good at. But NOW WHAT?

Let's look at verse **1 Corinthians 12:7**, "Now to each one the manifestation of the Spirit is given for the common good."

Another version of this verse states it slightly differently, but provides great perspective: "But the manifestation of the Spirit is given to every man to profit with."

If a gift were only for a man's own benefit, it would cease to be a "manifestation"—it would be sufficient for the person to possess the spirit consciously to himself. But the object of being His light is to give light to others. The object of the spiritual light is to help manifest to others.

Our motive should be serving the Lord. We should never use these gifts to manipulate others or to serve our self-interest.

Let's get real for a second…I can be honest with you, right?

When you are broken in every way, in heart, in health, but especially in finances; we instinctually look to the Lord for a blessing….a way out. We might even do things to help other, but only so that we can be recognized for doing them. Or even worse, we do things only to expect something in return. I think that is the point of what verse 7 is saying. That we should use our God given gifts and our motivation should be agape love.

> Doing good things, using our gifts simply because that is
> what we are supposed to do, and to always glorify the Lord in doing them.

- ✧ **Write down your top 3 gifts here. Share with the group. then beside each one, pray how the Lord will use them through you to glorify Him.**

# Day 2

**James 4:1-9**

I was listening to a Bethel sermon recently and the Pastor said something that lit up a light bulb for me. "God will always say YES to your request, unless it will harm you, or isn't in line with your mission."

I know that in my early Christian years, I was hesitant to ask for what I really wanted. I didn't want to seem selfish, or "waste God's time" with a request from little ole me. I blame my lack of knowledge of what scripture really says about our "wants". I didn't realize that our wants could actually be aligned with God's intentions!

He is a good good Father. He wants to bless us abundantly. But, as a good Father...He will not give you something, if you will get harmed or it could harm someone else.

> **\*Read 1 John 2:15- write down some things that you desire below.**

Would any of these things fill the hole that used to be there, or that may still exist in your heart? If not, take another crack at your list.

>   Don't worry about limits on the things that you ask for. Ask away!

There is a common misunderstanding of the Word and many people think that the Bible says that money is the root of all evil. Actually, what the Bible says is, "For the

Love of money is the root of all evil". See what I mean about how a lack of knowledge can take away our power and our blessings?

1 Timothy 6:10

I take the word of God literal. So, when it says, "on earth as it is in heaven". I believe that means we are intended to have all that we desire while still on Earth. After all, it doesn't say we have to wait until we die to live an abundant life.

There is nothing wrong with asking the Lord for what you really want. It says in Philippians 4:19: "And my God will meet all your needs according to the riches of his glory in Christ Jesus."

He knows what we need, and provides according to His glorious riches...

So start asking for what you want.

Now, sometimes we won't hear the answers that we want. Maybe it's because we aren't asking the right questions and talking about what God wants to talk about.

Let's look at Matthew 6:33.

Below write down your interpretation of what you think this verse means, or what it means to you.

"Seek ye first the Kingdom and HIS righteousness, and ALL these things will be added unto you."

Do you see? It means to set our hearts to pursue first and foremost, the display of God's dominion in every aspect of life that we have influence in. Set your heart and declare: if there is disease, it's gone; if there is torment, it's gone; and if there is conflict, there is restoration!

It's ALL about the dominion of ALMIGHTY God realized in the circumstances of life.

Have you seen the term "His righteousness" in your walk or study? Have you wondered what this meant, exactly?

"His righteousness" refers to the Christ like character in each of us. Be as Christ and set your heart for Him first.

One of my favorite songs is called "First" by Laura Daigle. Here are some of the lyrics that touch me: "Before I speak a word, let me hear your voice. And in the midst of pain, let me feel Your joy. I wanna know you. I wanna find you…in every season, in every moment."

So…get your heart right! Before you pick up your phone, computer, or newspaper; go find a quiet place to meet with Jesus. Talk with Him. Then ALL these things will be added unto you!

- ✧ **Share any longings that you have. Relate it to a "hole"**

# Day 3

**1 Peter 2:24-25**

Substitutionary atonement...what the heck is that? Try saying that 3 times really fast! The words look so complicated, don't they? I know it's not just me!

Our flesh and minds tend to make the word of God complicated...to twist them and we even complicate things to such a degree that we make our own theologies about what certain scripture mean.

I have always been the Jesus girl, who has taken the word of God literal from day one! To help with this one...substitutionary atonement refers to Jesus Christ dying as a substitute for sinners..so we wouldn't have to pay the ultimate price to atone for our own sins.. And thank you, Lord! Because we all know that each and every one of us are sinners! (Romans 3:9-18, 23).

> Christ died for our sins, in our place,
> so we would not have to suffer the punishment we deserve as sinners..

Let me make it really simple for you. The cross is our covenant. Through the cross (and the price paid), we are forgiven of all our sins and receive healing to our bodies. Isaiah 53:5, "by His wounds we are healed"; both spiritually and physically.

➢ **Think about a time where you prayed for something and it did not come to pass: healing, deliverance, a job. How did you feel?**

Complacency and ignorance of the Word enables some to tolerate unanswered prayers; including those prayers asking for healing. First, let me say this; Prayer is not our opportunity to "have our way" with the Lord. Prayer is our response to His invitation.

Hebrews 4:16, "Let us then approach God's throne of grace with _____, so that we _____ _____ _____ and find grace to help us in our time of _____."

Prayer is our chance to partner with Him, to help release His will and purposes on this Earth.

Do not believe what others may say…that we must tolerate sickness and pain because God uses it to build character in us. This is a direct violation of what Jesus taught and modeled.

And I don't know about you, but I refuse to sanctify anything that Jesus suffered to get rid of, especially to somehow exalt the process of disease.

We humans spend so much of our spiritual energy trying to fight for the things He already suffered to give us, instead of the things that have eternal significance.

Speaking of eternal significance, read Hebrews 9:28.

Is that good news or what? It goes on in Chapter 10 verse 5 to explain that Christ came to offer His body on the cross for us as the sacrifice; which was a completely acceptable penance, as deemed by God.

This isn't about keeping laws or even by not sinning. It is simply coming to Him in faith to be forgiven, and then follow Him in obedience.

- ✧ **So, why do you think we humans tolerate the absence of a "breakthrough" and not try to figure out why?**

Mark 9:14-29- This is a great example of tolerating the absence of a breakthrough. This child needlessly suffered his whole life due to lack of faith. Even when the disciples appeared, they couldn't heal the boy and repel the demon. But Jesus arrives on the scene and even confronts the boy's father, "'*If you can?*'", said Jesus. "Everything is possible for one who believes."

The disciples made the mistake of praying for the Kingdom to manifest through them…not IN them. They had the power all along within them, they just didn't believe.

A renewed mind knows and understands that sometimes the Lord wants to do stuff through us, not for us. When breakthrough's don't happen, we create theologies of why the breakthrough doesn't happen…You know, by saying things like,"It was just not God's time". We do this to insulate ourselves from the pain of an unanswered prayer

To circle back to prayer….

We have all been invited into the throne room. The Lord wants to interact with us, to talk with us, to help us. Many times, we don't know *what* to pray. We just know that in general people are supposed to be freed or healed and to be saved. But we have to believe and be focused and ask for specific direction to obtain a specific breakthrough.

We have been invited into the room with Jesus, so things do not remain the same. Praying has the power to changes things. Only when we really sacrifice...when we and fast and pray...is when we see the breakthroughs! But more on that next week.

For now, FOCUS.

Make time to speak with Jesus, get your day started down the right path each and every morning. This will open your life up to reason the blessings!

# Day 4

**Romans 15:18**

I want the end result of my life to be that others were obedient to Jesus Christ, in part because of my example. That was Paul's message and I can certainly relate!

Let's look at Romans 1:5, "Through Him and for His name's sake we received grace and apostleship to call people from among all Gentiles to the obedience that comes from faith."

- **Reflect and write down your personal evidence of God's grace in your life.**



- **Now recount times when you were blessed because of your obedience.**



There are many Christians who have a sincere faith, but don't see breakthroughs. The questions they often ask is, "Why Lord?".

When we come to the throne room, we should never be demanding of something; but rather, asking for something with grace...and to begin with what He wants to talk about.

We humans tend to humanize God. We forget about the power Jesus left us and suffered for. We feel limited because of our perception of the realm of human possibility. BUT, our assignment is to live in the realm of impossibility.

Our Lord is a supernatural God. We mustn't forget this as we go through our daily, normal lives.

Our battlefield is not in Iran or Iraq; it's not in another country or even down the street. The battlefield is in our minds.

Let's look at Ephesians 6:12.

"For our struggle is not against flesh and blood, but against the rulers, against the authorities, against the powers of this dark world and against the spiritual forces of evil in the heavenly realms."

I want you to reflect for a moment on your "thought life". How are your thoughts framed? Do you battle the powers of dark? Does your battle start first thing in the morning? Or does it hit you while you are lying in bed trying to fall asleep?

The enemy is real!

We must understand that we face a very real and powerful army, whose goal is to defeat Christ's church. The enemy will try to get you to forget the victory that has already been won. He will twist things are every opportunity to get you to see things from a dark lens. The enemy doesn't sleep...he just waits. He knows that something will happen to provide him a moment of weakness where we can slither in and cause chaos.

We know the enemy is real. We know that the war rages on and we have to have a battle plan in place to combat the attacks.

Christ gave us the tools to do this. It's all right there in the Bible and in the lessons that we have learned by studying the Word.

But do you open your toolbox every day?

Are you in the Word on a daily basis? The Word is the sword of the Spirit daily. Why wouldn't you have your sword ready to swing against the attacks?

Are you coming to the throne room, submitting in prayer?

Look, the battle you win in private becomes a public demonstration to all. We must learn our quiet place with God where we connect and contend for personal breakthrough. This is different for every person. You must find what works for you.

Too often we try to mimic the concepts and strategies of the public "miracle workers". Granted, sometimes there is success in these strategies, but they can't be maintained as part of a daily life. And we have to fight for consistency. And it has to come within each of us...if not, we (personally) won't have anything to give. After all, you cannot give what you do not have.

Our personal cry to God to increase our anointing comes upon us in our quiet place; and through us is released to overcome torment and illness. This is what is won in secret but demonstrated through us in public.

In private we are contending for a breakthrough.

Remember David's journey. He did not start out by conquering a giant. David began by killing a lion and bear when no one was watching. But it was these battles that qualified him to slay Goliath, under the very public display of a nation.

So when we pray and find strength in private, Heaven is backing us in public!

Go to Acts 14

Why do you think Paul and Barnabas decided to stay in Antioch for a long time?

I love that they stayed "there a long time"! I believe they decided to stay because there was a fight for a territory. And children in Christ are definitely fighters!

Another part of Acts 14 that I love is that Paul and Barnabas spoke BOLDLY! They spoke boldly because they believed…they had faith…and they knew that no one would follow them if they did not show strength.

The Lord is calling us to step out and step up…to speak the word BOLDLY! I want you to understand that God gave these men power to do great wonders, as confirmation of the message of grace. We too have this power…we just have to bold in showing our faith.

My whole point, is that we have to stop wasting time wishing for miracles. Instead, spend your time sowing seeds of faith on fertile ground the best that you can, with the gifts He has given you, and leave the final convincing up to the Holy Spirit.

# Day 5

**1 John 4:18**

I love the subject of fear. Fear is so powerful! And something that I struggled with most of my life. It started with little things like spider's and snakes. But then as I got older, my fears graduated from the fear of roller coasters and airplanes; to me getting sick, or my Mom getting sick, or death...the list could go on and on. Basically, I let fear enter my life at all stages.

In my early journey after I first became a Christian, I spent years fearing that I would reap consequences from the seeds that I had sown in the "old Rachel" year's...that God was going to strike me down for all the bad stuff that I had done (and trust me, there was plenty!)

If you remember from earlier in this study, I shared that in my early Christian years, I didn't know what I had in my hands...or understand any of it. I didn't yet have the knowledge of what I know now. Boy, oh boy...what a journey this has been so far!

But here is what I do know...everything you hear and receive in your life is filtered by either love or fear. We get to pick...we actually decide how we want to receive. We control our reaction or response to situations in life. And this can be motivated by love or it can be motivated by fear.

Again...I am going to say it...I love the subject of fear!

God knew that fear could be a huge game changer for many of us. But again, he armed us with the Word to fight this battle. Fear not (or similar verbiage) appears in scripture over 100 times (this varies depending on the translation that you study).

## "DO NOT FEAR"

Fear is one of the tools that the enemy uses to take us off of our path to abundance and blessings. When the Lord says DO NOT FEAR, He is exposing the tactics of the devil. Fear happens when we agree with the enemy. Anytime you believe a lie, you empower the liar. It is important that we are aware of the tactics of the enemy...and that we stop listening to the fear mongering and lies!

The Lord never told us to not fear to shame us or to expose what we are doing wrong; but to let us know that within reach is the grace to be victorious over fear.

When He commands, He empowers us to do what we thought we couldn't do.

## "DO NOT FEAR!"

Having an emotion of fear is not a sin, but partnering with the fear is. For example: when you happen to get a bad doctor's report, He isn't saying to deny the report. You should absolutely get things checked out. But what he is saying is that he has already suffered for you to be healed...so DO NOT FEAR.

Read Isaiah 51: 12-16.

> **Paraphrase this verse in your own words:**


⋄ **Think of the most fearful situation you have ever been in... or a fear that gets you worked up so much that you really start to believe the fear. What are your emotions?**

Read Psalm 118:6

Write down your interpretation of this verse.




Fear is a spirit, and the goal is to get that spirit off of us! But be ready, freeing yourself of fear is not for the faint of heart. But you can do this...

Draw strength from the great leaders in the Bible. Notice all of the times the Lord encourages them, "Do not fear for I am with you". Look to Joshua, Moses, or Esther?

2 Timothy 1 says, "For He didn't give us a _____ _____ _____ and timidity, but of _____, _____ and self-discipline."

All fear starts in the mind, and has a way working around in there until we are convinced that it is true.

But we are leaders in God. And we as leaders have a choice. We get to choose what kind of leader we will be.

Will we choose to lead in faith or lead in fear?

If you are going to be a leader, you must have a conviction. Conviction is knowing what's right and what's wrong, no matter what anyone else tells us. But we have the tools to gain great conviction. We have the Word of God, and as such we know what is right and what is wrong.


So, what is our number 1 tool to combat fear?

## LOVE!

What does the Word say about Love?

Go back and reread 1 John 4:18, "There is no _____ in _____!


The Word says, "perfect Love drives out fear". And we have the most perfect love possible...from God.

Those who don't know about the Love of God, will always fear punishment or repercussions...just like I used to back in the early days. And I even believe that most people who fear death, have fear because they literally don't know where they are going! They don't know Jesus. They think that all of their sins are sending them straight to Hell. But we can help them conquer this fear by sharing Jesus with them.

From One to One.


Do you see the big job that we have to do? All of the work still left to do?

"Beloved, those who are in Christ have no reason to fear the time of judgment", because we have been saved from punishment. Instead, we look forward to that day, because it will mean the end of sin and death!

Today, choose Love. If you have the spirit of fear on you, you don't get to operate in the spirit of power, love and self-discipline. But you do have a choice.

Choose Love.

FAITH WITHOUT WORKS IS DEAD

# Week 4

## *Faith Without Works Is Dead*

### Day 1

**Matthew 5:6**

I can bet most Christian's won't miss a meal this week, but I can guarantee most will miss many spiritual meals. In the beatitudes, Jesus gave us a code of "ethics" and a standard of conduct for all believers. At first glance, His words may seem to contradict each other. But I think that was the point. God's way of living usually is different than the "world's" God speaks in the eternal and our "normal world" speaks in the here and now. .

Look at Matthew 5:6.

I read this verse as, "You are blessed when you've worked up a good appetite for God. He's food and drink is the best meal you'll ever eat."

In this world, we have little hunger for God. Not many people will miss a meal during their week, but many will be missing Spiritual meals. We need both to live!

Blessed means, "happy, satisfied, content". So few of us are really blessed in the way Jesus talks about in Matthew 5. But we can be!

Let's talk about hunger...

Many of us experience hunger for food throughout out normal day. When do you start to get hungry? When you get hungry, how long before you satiate that grumbling belly? Maybe 20 minutes, if you are stuck in a meeting?

Really, do many of us really ever get hungry, hungry? Come on, you know that there is normally a snack within reach, or that dinner is only a few minutes away. The vast majority of people don't have to experience hunger. Food is everywhere!

But what about spiritual hunger? How often do you go without your spiritual meals? Do you go hours, days…maybe even weeks? And isn't our next spiritual meal just a thought away?

What if I told you that you could experience an amazing spiritual meal by sacrificing just a little bit of your food meals? Fasting can be an amazing tool to grow your relationship with God.

Now, I know what some of you are thinking, "Fasting? I can't go without food? My body *needs* food…andI love food!"

Yes, I know, the word "fasting" seems overwhelming; especially if you have never done it before. And it's true some people claim to fast from things from time to time…fasting from TV, or wine, or many other thing. But this is NOT fasting, as it was intended!

Fasting is abstaining from food.
And in doing so, you dethrone "King stomach" so you can hear the one true King!

In our culture of instant gratification, it's almost unheard of to ask people to sacrifice.

But sacrifice is necessary for growth!

Truth is, fasting isn't easy or fun in the beginning. But I am telling you from personal experience that fasting is THE MOST amazing *spiritual* experience! And let's not discount the huge health benefits that you can experience from fasting (way too many to share here right now!).

Contradictory to popular believe, fasting is NOT intended for the strong. It is for the weak and for people who desperately need to connect with the Savior. That is me!

I want more than anything to please my Papa up in Heaven! I can't talk enough about the benefits that fasting has brought into my life, both spiritually and physically. Fasting does not manipulate. Fasting gets you ready for God's answer. Fasting prepares your heart, for "not my will, but Yours be done". Fasting will literally change the way you see...well, Everything!

Fasting breaks you down and shifts you into a place of total obedience. When we begin to fast, we increase our receptivity to the Lord's voice. And clarity...oh, the clarity in which I Hear his voice now that I leverage the tool of fasting! Let's just say that I will continue to fast and will continue to know the direction He intends...with clarity!

Now, fasting is just an invitation. It is NOT required to have a relationship with God. It is something that is done voluntarily, in your time. But when you fast, you are saying, "Lord, I am breaking out of the routine of normal, giving up this food; I am sacrificing so as to come to you, Ready".

There is a mysterious connection that manifest between fasting and the Holy Spirit. When fasting, a special grace instantly comes upon you. You humble yourself before God; as if you are saying, "Lord, I need you." Fasting is an act of worship.

Romans 12:1-2, "Therefore, I urge you, brothers and sisters, in view of God's mercy, to offer your bodies as a living sacrifice, holy and pleasing to God—this is your true and proper worship. 2Do not conform to the pattern of this world, but be transformed by the renewing of your mind. Then you will be able to test and approve what God's will is—his good, pleasing and perfect will."

Fasting means to cover your mouth and refuse to eat. When you do, you will see God begin to do a deep spiritual work in your life. You will know when the time is right. God will call you to fast, you will feel a stirring in your heart.

Read Isaiah 55:1-2

People have been fasting and praying since Abraham. Moses fasted and prayed, often. Daniel fasted and prayed, often. Jesus fasted and prayed, often. They had a hunger for the Lord that was more driving than their hunger for food.

They didn't have donuts and ice cream or pizza. When they hungered, they fasted to be satiated by the Lord.

Today, people fill that hunger with food, sex, beer, drugs, the list goes on. This is our culture…it is the calling that we hear the loudest. Think about this…food costs money and last only a short time. But God offers us free nourishment that feeds our soul for eternity!

And how do we get it? We sit down, we shut up and we hang on! We seek Him.

There are some Christians who have a sincere faith, but have many frustrations in their walk. They can't hear the Word because of all of the noise!

Recently, I read a survey that was done of 100 people whom had sincere faith. They were asked what frustrates them the most about their walk. The top 5 list:


5. Inconsistent quiet time: "I know I should pray and read the Bible often. But sometimes my score is zero on effort. I know the right, I want the right, but I don't choose the right".

4. I feel along: "I don't sense God's presence with me. Even sometimes at church, I can't feel Him".

3. I don't measure up: "I have a nagging area of secret sin, anger, bitterness inside. I struggle with fear and anxiety."

2. Unanswered prayers: "I don't see any breakthroughs."

1. Prayers are cold and empty.

It's not that you don't want to change; it's just that you want other things more. I believe (well, I know from experience), that most of the time, we can't or won't do things because of the justifying story we tell ourselves. Mine story was, "If I don't eat first thing in the morning, I am going to rip someone's head off." Or, "I can't go without food…that can't be healthy!" Well, come to find out, neither was true.

- *So, what about you? What is the one thing about your Christian walk that frustrates you the most?

- Have you ever questioned why bad things happen? Is this an area of struggle in your life? Write down your thoughts…and really think about it.

Lay it all down. Then ask the Lord in prayer to take it all. All He asks of us is that we trust Him.

Read 1 John 5:1-5.

Many of our cries are, "Help me, Help me Lord", or "Why Lord, Why?" Jesus never promised that obeying Him would be easy. But the hard work and self-discipline of serving Christ is no burden to those who love him.

We want you to create a new habit. A new conversation, one that God would love to be having with you.

It goes like this: "I TRUST YOU LORD!!!"

It's not easy, but it's simple! And fasting and making this part of your Spiritual disciplines will not only change your life, but the lives of the ones you are standing in prayer for daily!

# *Day 2*

**John 6:61-65**

The design of this Bible study was birthed out of the transformation that happens when you become New. Shedding the old skin is the only way to receive new wine.

Let's look at Luke 5:36-39.

Jesus was such an awesome story teller and teacher! He knew He had to keep it simple sometimes with the misfit disciples He was hanging around. The wineskins were goatskin's sewn together at the seams to form a watertight bag. New wine would expand as it aged. So in order for it to age properly, it had to go into a new bag. If they put new wine into a used bag; the bag would burst and the new wine would be wasted.

Now, let's use that example to compare ourselves to the Pharisees. Remember the Pharisees were the ancient Jewish sect, who observed the strict traditions. The Pharisees were too stubborn to accept Jesus…they were old and established in their ways. And really, sometimes people just don't like change.

Can you think of any stubborn people? Maybe people who you know need Jesus, but they think that they will have to be controlled by an authority? Or they just don't want to change anything about themselves or their lives?

So think about the wine again. New wine expands as it ages. We, who are growing in knowledge and wisdom by His Word, are growing every day. We are new.

But, we cannot live into the promised abundant life while still wearing our old skins of mediocrity, shame, bitterness, un-forgiveness…and the list goes on and on.

When we become new, we also will have new traditions, new approaches and some new disciplines...many "news" that we never would have been able to imagine before. But, as always...He provides tools to help us grow.

The next tool that I want to discuss is meditation. Meditation is one of the most important Spiritual disciplines that we should incorporate into our everyday lives.

What is meditation, exactly?

Well, meditation is simply calming the mind, becoming silent and finding a state of deep peace. Sounds pretty good, doesn't it! Plus the benefits are too numerous to cover in this study, but we will touch on a couple.

Let's start with the health benefits of meditation. With meditation you will realize improved mood and working memory, you'll alleviate stress, increase the size of your brain! (for real?); and enhance the strength of your immune system. Those benefits alone are worth 15 minutes of your day!

All wellness and sickness start in your mind. Meditating daily will help you keep a steadfast mind! There are a ton of resources out there on how to begin meditating. The best way to start that I know of is to find an awesome yoga teacher and start doing yoga. After all, yoga is just moving meditation. It is about the mind, body connection and your breath is the bridge to them both.

While doing yoga, you focused on our breath. It is amazing how this quiets the chatterbox in our minds. And as an added bonus...yoga adds in its own health benefits, such as flexibility, strength and overall health. So many health benefits to yoga, but also is for another book!

Now, how do we tie the tool of meditation to our spiritual journey?

Here is the definition of Christian meditation: Christian meditation is a form of prayer in which a structured attempt is made to become aware of and reflect upon the revelations of God.

The word meditation comes from the Latin word meditārī, which has a range of meanings including: to reflect on, to study and to practice. The Greek word for meditation is: Stochasmos, which means: thinking, thought, reflection.

So, we use meditation to:

- ✓ Provide structure to establish our time with God
- ✓ Practice control and awareness (through breathing)
- ✓ Reflect on current situations
- ✓ Pray for resolution, support, blessings, direction
- ✓ Quiet our minds so we can hear His voice

In a nutshell...

When you don't know what to pray, don't worry; the Spirit does. When you are "stuck", just use other tools like the Word of God to help guide your reflection. Then just listen! You will be amazed at the voice you hear when open your heart to hear

Remember our weapons? We are well equipped to tear down any strongholds in our lives, but most of us don't find them important enough to use.

> *Read: Joshua 1:8, Psalm 1:2, Isaiah 26:3, Psalm 119:148. Do you see any similarities? Below, write down all the similarities in these verses.**

Now, reflect on what are you going through right now. Do you need a revelation? Open up that Bible; find out what the word has to say about your current and start meditating and praying those scriptures!

Meditation and Fasting…two of the most effective ways to God in an amazing way!

Read 2 Timothy 2:15.
◇ **Be honest, how did you feel after reading this?**

To me, I felt inadequate, over-whelmed, and a little scared! It sounds like a lot of pressure! But, let me remind you...even those of us that have been on this walk for a long time still struggle to have a steadfast mind!

The enemy is strong.

But what does the word say? The word of God tells us how to live for Him and serve Him. You can do this! Don't be one of those "believers" who ignore the Bible. One day, those folks will have some explaining to do!

Extra Tool for Your Toolbox:

The Simple 5 Step Process - to help you develop the discipline of meditation.

1. Read it!

Read it: Read the verse several times; look for key phrases and words. Focus on what you read and what it may mean. Think of other ways to say it. Notice how specific words may be emphasized and how that affects the meaning of the verse.

2. Write it:

Write the verse out exactly as it is written; close your Bible so you don't get distracted by other verses. Write a small phrase, and go to the next step—say it. Write down any insights, thoughts, and revelations. Write the phrase several times. Writing the Word opens something that reading doesn't always open in our understanding; it can be powerful and profound.

3. Say it!

Say the verse aloud—loud enough to hear yourself. "Faith comes by hearing, and hearing by the word of God" (Rom. 10:17). As you repeat Scripture phrases, certain words will leap out at you. Repeat these words quietly before the Lord as your heart connects with His through His living Word.

4. Sing it!

Singing is a means to unlocking the heart. Sing your phrase several times. Write down what you sense and perceive. Our singing voices function in a way distinct from other musical instruments. No other instrument can carry a flow of thought and melody. Declaring Bible verses in song impacts our spirit, soul, and body in a dynamic way. And God has ordained that our singing to Him would move His heart too.

5. Pray it!

Prayer is a God-ordained means of communing with God. When you repeat a phrase and believe it, you're speaking it to God, which is prayer. As you pray your verse, ask the Lord to help you believe it. If a phrase invites faith or obedience to walk it out, ask God to help you live it out.

When we meditate on the Word, we use the Bible to encounter God. We experience more of His love, understand His truth, and come to know Him more intimately.

If you really want to know God in a deeper way, then invest time in doing these spiritual disciplines.

# Day 3

**Ephesians 6:10-20**

In Philippians 4:6 Paul says, "Don't worry about anything; instead, pray about everything." Don't be anxious...just pray! Pray about everything! Pray and petition, with thanksgiving; present your request to God. Paul was in a Roman prison when he wrote this letter. He wrote the letter to his brothers and sisters in faith to thank them for their gift and to encourage them in their faith. Sitting in prison...Paul was encouraging others. Can you just picture what the Roman prison was like back then? There were no basketball courts, or weight rooms, or television. I picture him shackled, sitting in filth. Hungry. Thirsty
Yet, he is writing letters of encouragement, telling them to REJOICE...always!

If I were to think of one word for this letter it would be Joy. Paul was saying that his joy was not dependent upon his circumstances or other people. But his joy was from Jesus.

➢ **Read Philippians 1. Yes, the whole chapter. I want you to think of a time you may not have been in jail or prison literally, but maybe a in a situational prison, or prison of thoughts? Where did you go for guidance?**

✧ **Now, go back to week 1, day 4. Did you want to answer, "phone a friend"? See, you had a history; but now it's time to build a new history.**

The goal at the end of this study is for you to understand that your first action should always be to your knees; even when face down. You must surrender total control of any situation where you feel you are drowning...surrender it to God.

This will be hard at first, because we have spent most of our lives trying to carry all the weight ourselves. Or worse yet, leaning hard on another poor soul who wanted to help, but had no idea what to say to us.

I like to paraphrase Philippians 4:6 by say, "If you are going to pray, don't worry. But if you are going to worry, don't pray."

The Greek word for everything is, EVERYTHING.

The Word doesn't tell us to only pray about the easy task or for the things that you may not be able to handle. He wants you to lay it all at his feet. The good, the bad and the ugly!

I want you to start to journal. Don't over think this. A journal is just a tool to use so that you can start to see your areas of growth and the areas where you still struggle. This can also be an awesome tool and testimony that you can show others.

To get started...begin with writing down all your worries.

Start to journal every day. Also, capture any insights that you're getting from this journey. The Lord is communicating with you all day long. Writing in your journal is another way for you to "quiet down" to receive His messages. We are going to get more into journaling tomorrow...but start today!

This short Bible study was designed to be a rigorous Spiritual training for the purpose of Godliness. There are many spiritual disciplines or tools, but I covered the ones that I feel are the most important for your spiritual growth.

Study of Scripture, Praying, Fasting, Meditating and Journaling

My goal for you as you turn the last page of this study, that you are FREE from bondage! Using these tools will change you. And with continued use will help you live out the victoriously abundant life your Papa in Heaven has written just for you.

Now, back to the very basics...Prayer.

Prayer is simply a conversation with God. According to many sources, Christians have stated that they pray an average of 5 minutes a day. We all know that we should pray, we really want to pray, and we all believe. But we are just really bad at the actual practice.

One of the reasons I fast is because while in the quiet fasting state, the Holy Spirit takes over my prayer life. The spirit tugs at me to pray...so I do. And this tug spills into my everyday life. I truly is amazing that when you start your day by setting the expectations (and starting in positivity of prayer), that the rest of your day lines right up!

Remember Matthew 6:33, "Seek first the kingdom and His righteousness."

The best way to form this habit of daily prayer is just to do it. But some great advice that I heard Denzel Washington share: "Put your shoes way underneath your bed. Doing that will ensure you have to hit your knees when you wake up."

It can be as simple as little grateful prayers like, "Thank you, Lord for this day! Thank you for my breath, my health" or whatever blessing comes to mind.

And then I always ask that He lead me all day long.

It can really be that simple. There is absolutely no value in making this complicated (remember, we already talked about that!)

My yoga time is a time that I spend praying. I am usually in a fasting state, and really connected. For me, I have found this the most beneficial. The spirit is leading me through those prayers.

The little breath prayers are a part of my daily routine also. You know, you are on Facebook, and you see prayer request after prayer request? I just stop and say a small prayer. I don't just click "like" and move on. If I see a prayer request, you can bet I am praying. I would want people to pray for me. Remember, don't overthink this. Let the spirit take over!

# Day 4

**John 13:35**

We are nearing the end of our journey together and I can't help but wonder if this study made a difference in your life.

Do you feel any different? Has your perspective changed?

I believe that if you came into this study hungry, that you will leave satisfied. Remember living water? You shall thirst NO MORE!

Before we end our walk together...let's talk a little bit more about love.

I am going to be totally transparent with you. I know, shocker!

But I struggled with this Love thing. I wanted to love, who I wanted to love. I wanted it to be totally my choice.

I was one of those judging Christians. Pointing fingers at those who were still doing what I used to do. The pot smoker's wasting through their days...the drinkers who made every single holiday a day where their alcoholism went unnoticed.

I can tell you, I did not disciple very many people in that time in my life. No surprise there, right! You can't provide out of lack!

If you haven't figured this out yet, Christians are historically the worst at persecuting. Christians will be the ones who will point out all of your faults…when you cuss, when you lose your composure, or when you may or may not have walked on water and almost drowned a chubby, bully kid at the local pool. (OK, maybe that last reference was just my example!)

Gandhi has been quoted as saying, "It is not your Jesus I have a problem with, but your Christians who are so unlike your Jesus." OUCH! The truth really does hurt.

Jesus spoke of love in John 13:35 and what he expected from us, when he said, "Your love for one another will prove to the world that you are my disciples."

So, do people see us bitter towards others? Bickering between the pews? Or do they see us loving one another.

It is time that we stop looking at one another as rivals, but as teammates. Love is NOT a feeling, but an attitude that displays itself in action.

Read 1 Corinthians 13

Now it's time for some spiritual and moral inventory. And be honest.

> **When you give, do you go and tell others? Are you secretly thinking about how you are going to be blessed?**

Let me just say that when bought someone's lunch, or gave the beggar on the highway money, that was your blessing. Boasting about the act to others steals away that blessing.

Reference Matthew 6:3, "But when you _____ to _____ _____ _____, don't let your left hand know what _____ _____ _____ is doing."

Jesus was talking about our motives in this verse.

Are you motives pure? Are you giving to be recognized or to get something back? Or are you giving, because it's the right thing to do? And you do if freely.

Why do you give?

Let me share a few of verses of my own message…..

> *If I can run a 4-minute mile, but not have love*
> *If I can heal others diseases using my gift, but not have love*
> *If I know the word, from Genesis to Revelation, but not have love*
> *If I am a Billionaire, living life on my terms, but not have love*
> *If I am the greeter at my church doors, but not have love*
> *I HAVE NOTHING.*

⋄ **Take a minute and paraphrase your own list, as I have above. Make it personalized to your life right now.**

Now, I want you to re-read 1 Corinthians 13:4-8. Which verse or verses can you personally resonate with you?

Mine is always perseveres. Love always perseveres. The fact that I am still married, is such an awesome testimony to "Love always perseveres". The first couple years of our marriage were ROUGH! Before Jesus, and without His love, I would have run for the hills like I had in previous situations. But together we got through those early years.

But then came years 8-10. These were also very challenging, but in a different way. We dealt with my husband's mercury poisoning, the suicide of my big brother, the sudden death of a great friend and business partner, my own 4-month long illness…But we stuck it out! We persevered. And now we are reaping the fruits of those labors! All through His glory!

For the life of me, I don't understand why people choose to continue to suffer and go through life without Jesus.

Choose Love.

Now, here is one where I struggled.

Go to 1 John 4:19-21. Read these verses aloud.

I saw this struggle not only in myself, but in other Christians.

So...here is an example of where I struggled with this one. Many, many years ago, I had these crazy neighbors. It made me think of how it must have been living next to Ozzy Osborne and his family. Just chaos, all of the time.

When we first moved, we would chat with these crazy neighbors from time to time. On one occasion, the husband shared about a time when he took all of the seats out of his van, put a mattress down in the back and drove over to the next town (20 miles away) to go to a drive in movie. He then continued to share that the next time he intended on taking his kids! We are kids of different ages, but at least one, under the age of 5.

Now, I am a mom...for the life of me, I couldn't wrap my head around how this guy would put his little kids in the back of his van, unsecured...on top of a loose mattress...and drive 20 miles away to go to the movies. My mom-protection mode kicked into overdrive!

I won't share the words that went through my mind at the time, because they were not very Christian. But I did say (in my mind), "The Hell you will!"

From that moment on, I was that judging fool from next door. I noticed everytime their 4-year-old daughter took off down the road on her bike in her pajamas, or when their boys would climb into the car and rev up the engine. I judged and judged and judged. It got so back that I wouldn't allow my kids to play or hang out with them at all.

There was no room for Love with all of the Judgement I was slinging around!

Contrast that to where I am now. I can now see that those kids acted out just because they were starving for attention. But their parents were just so wrapped up in their lives that their kids get left behind in all of the busy times and chaos. The dad never, ever played ball with his kids. The kids were always outside while the parents were always inside.

The chaos and neglect never changed…but my response to it did. I chose a different path. Instead of judging, I took action out of love.

One morning I saw the oldest boy walking to the bus stop. He was probably going to miss the bus, which he did almost every day. The chair that I sit in to do my morning Bible Study faces out of our big picture window, so I had a pretty clear view of the activities.

The boy was walking with his head down; presumably just with the thought of having to tell his parents that he missed the bus again.

As I watched this, I was taken over by a sense of compassion for the boy. I immediately began to pray for him. I prayed for him, his family, his mom and dad, his siblings…I prayed hard for them all.

Over the next few weeks I continued to pray for that family. And don't you know that I started to see the Mom outside throwing baseball with her sons. Then the husband followed suit. I watched from that big bay window and saw those people become a family again. I am telling you…prayer works!

I now have a love for that family, and pray for them often.

The Lord needed to prune me of all of that judgment. I had to get rid of all of that baggage in order for Him to propel me. No way was He going to release me to effect many lives, If I wasn't loving His children. All of his children!

Remember, like we talked about earlier…you have to have life in order to give life. And, you produce what you carry. God loves me too much to leave me the same.

In order for the Lord to do work IN you and THROUGH you, we must first get rid of the strongholds. Prune all of those thorny limbs…smooth those jagged edges.

God is doing something significant in and through me right now. He is using me to reach others, so that I can help them allow God to do something significant in and through THEM!

Wise women that we need to let go of those things that hold us back. As long as you continue to hold onto these things, it will become your future.

I don't know about you, but I know that Jesus suffered to eradicate my past!

I will not let his sacrifice have been in vain!

"IF EVER THERE COMES A TIME WHEN THE WOMEN OF THE WORLD COME TOGETHER PURELY & SIMPLY FOR THE BENEFIT OF MANKIND, IT WILL BE A FORCE THE WORLD HAS NEVER KNOWN."

# Final Day

## "If Ever There Comes a Time When the Women of the World Come Together Purely & Simply for the Benefit of Mankind, It Will be a Force the World Has Never Known."

Let this last day together be your anointing…your send off into battle if you will.

You have studied hard and completed the training over these past 4 weeks. I am so proud of you!

You now have all the weapons you need to grow and continue your walk. But you are also empowered to GO out…touch people's lives, reach other women, help them develop their prowess and help nurture more disciples!

➢ Read James 2:14-26. Now go look up "intellectual assent". Write the definition in space below.

✧ Where do you fall in between these two lines?

True Faith                                Intellectual Assent

If you are somewhere in the middle or closer to the right, let's try to close that gap! Some people who claim to have faith, actually only have intellectual assent. To me intellectual assent means that a person has made a decision in their head to believe, but they haven't committed their heart to faith. And this leaves them with an incomplete faith.

True faith transforms not only our minds, but our conduct and our entire lives. If our lives remain unchanged, we don't truly believe the truths we claim to believe.

Faith + Action = REAL TRUE FAITH

We cannot earn our salvation by obeying and serving the Lord. These things show that our commitment to Him is real. But these things are just a manifestation and confirmation of our faith in Christ.

Jesus came to serve, not be served. What does that look like in your life right now?

Let us do an experiment. Write down your day from the minute you wake up, until you lay your head down at night. Go ahead, do it right now.

What is your day centered around? You? Your kids? Your career?

If you can honestly look at your life and say, "I am a servant leader", than congratulations! I am so proud of you! But many of us still fall short.

I had to work really hard to become a servant leader, and I work hard everyday to continue to be that servant leader.

If you are not serving, that is very likely blocking blessings that God has for your life.

Please hear my heart; I am not saying serve so that you will be blessed. I am saying serve because that is what we are called to do. Our job is to serve. It pleases our Father in Heaven when we serve. We don't serve to get something out of it...but remember, God is a Father that provides for his children.

>As you sow, so shall you reap.

The goal of this whole study is for our Father in Heaven and the world to look at us and say, "You look so much like Jesus".

That is how we win souls, my friends!

# *Homework*

Here is my homework for you! **Start a Bible study** in your home. Invite your friends and start growing in the Word.

I do hope you take part in our nationwide virtual Bible study! We will bring together the masses and grow together in His Word!

More information can be found on our website: www.women-at-the-well.org.

Can you imagine a whole bunch of Godly women, all fired up on a video conference growing together in our faith? That is how we change the world...together, reaching out to one person at a time! I am so excited to continue this journey with you and those that your story brings to the Well.

There are souls out there in need of love and help. Let us be their example!

It has been such an awesome experience to write this study. I have grown so much from digging more into the Word. In writing this, I imagine that I am almost experiencing it right along with you; as you hold it in your hands.

Have faith and patience in yourself on your walk and for yourself.

What was once a shut in, no people liking, narcissist...is now a Jesus loving, people loving, disciple who wants nothing more than to see you shine full in the glory of the Lord.

Be sure to check out the other resources on our website, especially our "No make up, No filter, No Bull" blog...plus all of the other Bible studies available to you!

As always…I don't know you, but I love you!

*Rachel*

> *Go be great! Rise up, and lean in to get everything that God has for you!*

Stay connected:
Website: www.racheltucker.org

Facebook: https://www.facebook.com/championsforchrist/

Twitter: Fitgrl09

Instagram: Championmaker

Youtube: Rachel Tucker

Email: crtministries@gmail.com

*Request Rachel to Speak*

*Women's Ministry, Students, Churches, Retreats, Conferences,*

*Leadership Events*

©copyright 2016 Rachel Tucker

www.racheltucker.org

©copyright 2016 All rights reserved. This book is protected by the copyright laws of the United States of America. This book may not be copied or reprinted for commercial gain or profit. The use of short quotations or occasional page copying for personal or group study is permitted. Persmission will be granted upon request.

Edited by: Robin Housley

Made in the USA
Columbia, SC
01 September 2017